ZOOBABIES

ZOOBABIES

PHOTOGRAPHS BY MICHAEL O'NEILL

TEXT BY CAROLYN FIRESIDE

A CONSTANCE SULLIVAN BOOK

VILLARD BOOKS

NEW YORK
1991

All rights reserved under International and Pan-American Copyright Conventions. Published in the United States by Villard Books, a division of Random House, Inc., New York, and simultaneously in Canada by Random House of Canada Limited, Toronto. Villard Books is a registered trademark of Random House, Inc.

Planned, prepared and produced by Constance Sullivan Editions, New York.

Library of Congress Cataloging-in-Publication Data

O'Neill, Michael

   Zoobabies / Michael O'Neill

     p. cm.

   ISBN 0-679-40698-0

   1. Zoo animals.   2. Animal—Infancy.   3. Zoo animals—Pictorial works.   4. Animals—Infancy—Pictorial works.   I. Title.

QL77.5.054 1991

636.088'9—dc20   91-50271

9 8 7 6 5 4 3 2

First Edition

Manufactured in the United States of America

For Muni and Violet

PREFACE

While working on this book I had the rare and unforgettable
experience of being enclosed in a small room, one-on-one, with some
amazing wild creatures. Many of them were endangered species, bred
in captivity and tenderly cared for by humans.

I began taking these pictures by visiting zoos around the country
and improvising a studio with a paper or canvas backdrop. When the
baby animal was brought in, we hoped he or she would sit for a
portrait. Sometimes it worked, sometimes it didn't. I never knew what
to expect. A tiger snarled from only a foot away, an alligator jumped
high off of the floor, and an orangutan wouldn't let go of my camera.
As I do when making any portrait, I tried to find the essential
characteristics of each personality.

Some animals allowed me to get much closer than others. The
koala was perfectly at ease, even when our noses were almost
touching. But the armadillo was always in motion, skittering across
the set in search of a hole to disappear into. The cats were awesome
because although they're babies, they're still "big cats" and their roars
are terrifying. Wildest of all was the leopard. Chubby, the pygmy
hippo, kept opening his gigantic mouth and charging. Although the
giraffe was only three weeks old, he was about seven feet tall and
made facial expressions reminiscent of cartoon characters. You don't
realize how long a giraffe's tongue is until you stare up into his face—
it seems to go on forever. Young as the bear was, I sensed his wildness,
and, when photographing two male wolf cubs who were littermates, I
noticed one was shy, while his brother was forward and aggressive.

In each encounter I was aware of dealing with an individual,
unique to its species, complete with moods, attitudes, likes, and
dislikes. I hope my pictures capture some of the sense of wonder and
pleasure I felt in getting to know these zoo babies.

Michael O'Neill

CINCO

Reticulated Giraffe (*Giraffa camelopardalis reticulata*)
Male
Born May 4, 1991
Lives in the savannahs of sub-Saharan Africa

Born six feet tall and reaching heights of nearly twenty feet, giraffes use their superior size to select the finest leaves from treetops and shrubs. This nutritional advantage guarantees them plentiful and healthy offspring. When a calf is threatened, a single kick from its mother's powerful front hooves can kill a lion. Every giraffe's markings are unique, like human fingerprints, enabling them to recognize each other and make friends for life.

CODA

Timber Wolf (*Canis lupus*)
Male
Born April 10, 1991
Lives in forests of Europe, Asia, and North America

The marathon runner of the animal world, this close kin of the domestic dog can track its prey at speeds of thirty miles per hour for over twelve miles before slowing to a trot. Intelligent and social beasts who mate for life, timber wolves live in cooperative packs and share responsibility for hunting, defense, and caring for their young.

PENNY

Lowland Gorilla (*Gorilla gorilla*)
Female
Born May 3, 1989
Lives in rainforests of West and Central Africa

Penny will share sleeping quarters with her mother until she's three, when she'll be grown up enough to have her own cozy nest of twigs and branches. Even as an adult she travels with her mother's troop of females and their young, led by an older male called the silverback. Highly intelligent and peace loving, gorillas never prey, and resort to physical violence only in defense, when all else fails.

DAKIN

Koala (*Phascolarctos cinereus*)
Male
Born August 17, 1988
Lives in the forests of eastern Australia

Perhaps the earliest endangered species, koalas have been protected by man since 1898. The gourmets of the animal world, they're very choosy about their menus, eating only certain varieties of eucalyptus leaves. Since they sleep eighteen hours a day and use their nights to search for food, koalas have little time to socialize. They'd much prefer to snooze after a fine supper, tucked comfortably into their favorite resting fork, high in the trees.

VIOLET

Nubian Ibex (*Capra ibex nubiana*)
Female
Born April 15, 1991
Lives in high altitudes of Africa
Endangered

Baby Violet will grow up to boast impressive, backward-sweeping horns, a brownish coat, and almost twice as many taste buds as a human, which make all sorts of leaves and grasses simply delicious. A surefooted cousin of the goat, the ibex has been endangered since man invented firearms, and today lives principally in captivity.

ABRAMS

Nine-banded Armadillo (*Dasypus novemcinctus*)
Male
Born March 1991
Lives in savannas and deserts of southern United States

The nine-banded armadillo's horny body plating, or carapace, traps warm day air, providing heat on chilly desert nights. Its skunklike secretion discourages approachers, and its long snout and sticky tongue are perfect tools for trapping insects. When endangered, the armadillo simply rolls itself into an armored ball that is invulnerable to attack.

Sumatran Orangutan (*Pongo pygmaeus*)
Male
Born March 22, 1986
Lives in dense rainforests on the island of Sumatra
Endangered

These reddish-brown, shaggy-haired tree dwellers, second largest of the great apes, are the only species found outside Africa. Fierce-looking when mature but winsome, they live alone or in small groups of mothers and their young. Their food of choice is fruit, their favorite lounging spot a tree-house sleeping loft, comprised of branches and constructed nightly. Since the orangutans' solitary lifestyle and peaceful nature make them easy prey for animal and human predators, they are now almost extinct.

 JATI

Indian Elephant (*Elephas maximus*)
Female
Born in the wild (birthdate unknown)
Lives in forests of Asia
Endangered

Because their massive weight is so well distributed, Indian elephants can steal silently through the bush, leaving almost no tracks. They use their tusks, actually giant teeth, to prise bark from bamboo trees or wield as weapons. When threatened or abused, these docile creatures will charge at speeds faster than a human sprints—about fifteen miles an hour. Courting males and females caress each other with their trunks and walk together, trunks entwined, as if holding hands.

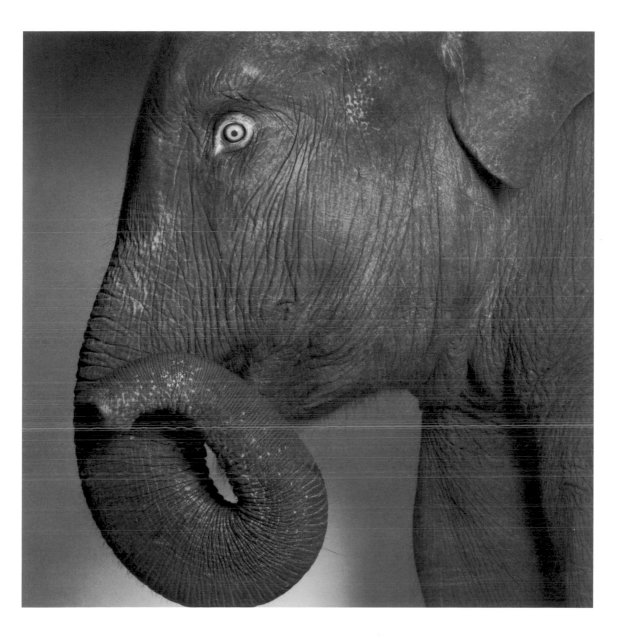

MOSHI

Tawny Owl (*Strix aluco*)
Male
Born April 12, 1991
Lives in deciduous forests and open woodlands of North
America, Europe, and northwest Africa

Denizens of the dark who are blinded by sunlight, tawny owls feed at night on a variety of prey, from worms to barnyard fowl, from fish to roe deer. By day, they hide in holes or in thick foliage, protected by their plumage coloration. The tawny owl rarely builds its own nest, but settles comfortably into other creatures' quarters, including birdhouses and garages.

BOURÉE

White Alligator (*Alligator mississippiensis*)
Male
Born September 1990
Lives in the rivers, swamps, and bayous of
southeastern United States

Alligators' legendary size and deadliness have made them the
sharks of Southern folklore. Actually, they flee at the very
sight of human beings. Blue-eyed Bourée is white because his
skin lacks pigment. He can get sunburned and, because he has
no camouflage, would be easy prey in the wild. He and
seventeen of his male nestmates are the only white alligators
known to man.

SANDIA

Mountain Tapir (*Tapirus pinchaque*)
Male
Born February 1, 1991
Lives in the mountains of South America
Endangered

Although the tapir may resemble a pig or an elephant, its closest relatives are actually the rhino and the horse. Almost identical to the *tapirus* of twenty million years ago, tapirs are masters of survival. They can swim, dive, and scramble up mountains with equal skill. They feed on roots and plants at night when browsing's safest. This baby's dappled coat, a natural camouflage, will fade and become one solid color by the time he's grown.

CHUBBY

Pygmy Hippopotamus (*Choeropsis liberiensis liberiensis*)
Male
Born February 26, 1991
Lives near rivers and lakes of African grasslands

Although their battles resemble welterweight boxing matches and last for hours, pygmy hippos would rather spend the day sunning on a river bank, lolling in the water, or wallowing in mud baths that rid them of skin parasites. Their almost hairless bodies give off organic sunblock, an oily substance that prevents burning and helps heal sores and wounds. Hippos are surprisingly light eaters who snack at night on grasses, then head back to the shore. Their favorite form of exercise is yawning.

BESAR

Sumatran Tiger (*Panthera tigris sumatrae*)
Male
Born March 26, 1991
Lives in the forests and swamps of Sumatra
Endangered

The Sumatran tiger is one kitty who loves water. He's a frequent visitor at drinking spots and, on hot days, stands or lies in streams to keep cool. A stealthy, solitary, and silent hunter, he'll cover up to twelve miles a night searching for prey. Largest of the big cats, adult Sumatran tigers measure over eight feet from head to tail-tip and weigh in at almost four hundred pounds.

PATCHES

Cape Hunting Dog (*Lycaom pictus*)
Male
Born March 9, 1991
Lives in the deserts and savannahs of Africa
Endangered

Ferocious, with a battle-scarred appearance, the Cape hunting dog cannot be tamed. This vanishing breed lives in close-knit packs, hunts in squads numbering as high as sixty, and willingly shares kills. Like a football team, the squads use superb cooperation, taking turns in the chase and a combined attack to bring down prey much larger than themselves, like wildebeests and zebras.

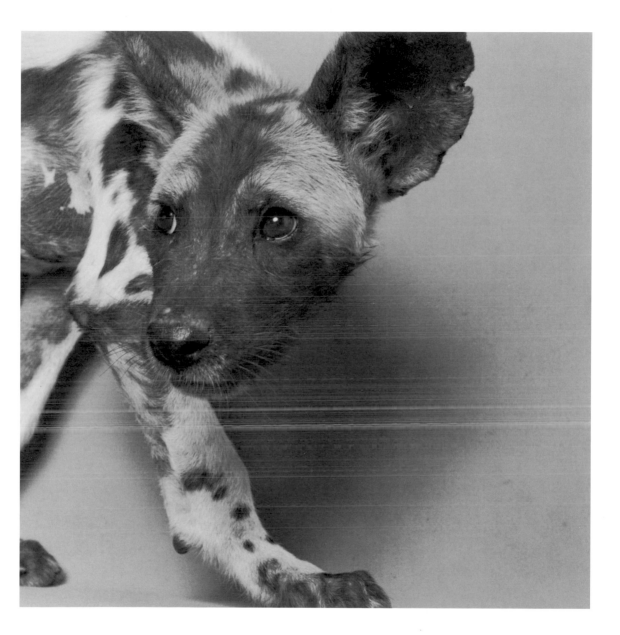

KWANZA

Black Rhinoceros (*Diceros bicornis*)
Female
Born October 3, 1990
Lives in the bush, forests, plains, and semideserts of Africa
Endangered

Black rhinos have been on earth for at least three million years. These easygoing vegetarians are really gray, although their color is determined by the mud in which they love to wallow. Their reputation for blind charging actually results from their eyes being placed on the sides of their heads, which prevent them from focusing with accuracy. The mature black rhino's horns are actually masses of hair fused together.

MISTY

Cinnamon Bear (*Ursus americanus cinnamomus*)
Female
Born January 10, 1990
Lives in forests and woodlands of western United States
and Canada

In good weather, these intelligent and private creatures are forever on the prowl, searching for the most succulent food available—from nuts and fruit to fish and barnyard fowl. During the coldest months they snooze in a cozy den, out of harm's way. Smaller and shyer than their grizzly relatives, cinnamon bears, whose ancestors were dogs, live singly or with their young and like to do their scavenging by moonlight. Except for the occasional dash for prey, they lead an easygoing life.

MUNI

European Roe Deer (*Capreolus capreolus*)
Female
Born May 8, 1991
Lives in the temperate forests of Eurasia

This tiny fawn will eventually lose her markings, alternating a
solid russet summer coat with a gray-brown winter one. The
smallest of her species, she's a nighttime forager for leaves and
fruit. The foot glands of roe deer imprint scent trails, and
during courtship they leave figure-eight-shaped tracks called
"roe rings," formed when a male pursues a female.

BESS

Chapman's Zebra (*Equus burchelli chapmanni*)
Female
Born July 25, 1990
Lives in the grasslands and savannahs of East Africa

Why zebras have stripes is an unsolved mystery, but it's only one of several puzzling things about them. Although they graze by moonlight while their enemies sleep, they spend the day lounging unprotected in the open, where lions on the prowl can't miss them. Zebras move in close-knit herds, yet often join up with a traveling band of ostriches or wildebeests. Only they know whether it's for company, variety, or camouflage.

DREYFUS

Lion (*Panthera leo*)
Male
Born October 1, 1990
Lives in the savannahs of Africa

These lordly beasts are such expert predators they can afford
to sleep away two-thirds of their days. Unlike other big cats,
who are loners, lions live in prides of several mature males
and up to fifteen females and their young. Teams of females
do the hunting while healthy males stay at home to guard
against invaders. Larger than females and more awesome
because of their lush manes and terrifying roars, adult males
are always the first to feed off the lionesses' kill.

PATRIOT

Black-footed Penguin (*Spheniscus demersus*)
Male
Born January 22, 1991
Lives in the seas off South Africa

Always dressed for a night on the town, penguins are
definitely urbanites whose colonies number up to a million
inhabitants. Their favorite foods are gourmet seafood delicacies
like squid and shrimp. Dedicated family birds who mate for
life, they return each year to the same nesting site and can
pick out their own chicks in a crowd of young.

GOBLIN

Siamang Gibbon (*Hylobates syndactylus*)
Male
Born October 30, 1990
Lives in the mountain forests of Malaysia and Sumatra

Fruit lovers who dwell in trees, these amazingly acrobatic two-foot-tall apes not only swing from bough to bough but also hang from and walk upright along branches. Siamang couples serenade each other with beautiful duets, and both care for their offspring until, at three, they're old enough to start a family of their own.

SLEEPING BEAUTY

Pot-bellied Pig (*Sus scroea*)
Female
Born January 1, 1991
Lives in Vietnam and China

For thousands of years, these living, breathing, oinking little piggy banks have been prized as pets (and food) in Asia. But not until 1985 did the pot-bellied pig capture America's heart, even appearing on talk shows! Good-natured, clean, and eager to please, Sleeping Beauty can be taught to heel, tumble, fetch, and obey. She's easier to housebreak than a dog, expresses affection with a nuzzle of her sensitive snout, and loves nothing better than a good, old-fashioned tummy rub.

MARIAH

Asian Spotted Leopard (*Panthera pardus*)
Female
Born July 1, 1990
Lives in trees of southern Asian rainforest
Endangered

A shy and wily carnivore, the spotted leopard has no roar. Her patterned coat blends into the forest's thick, sun-dappled foliage and makes her practically invisible—until she pounces on a deer or swats a bird or monkey. She spends her days and nights sleeping on a high tree branch and only hunts at twilight.

MAYA

Arabian Oryx (*Oryx leucoryx*)
Female
Born March 28, 1991
Lives in the African Sahara
Endangered

A resourceful nomad, the Arabian oryx is perfectly designed
for desert life. Its white coat, heavier in winter, absorbs the
sun's rays and provides extra warmth. In summer, the hooves
and horns are used to scrape out cool and shady resting places
under bushes or beside dunes. Extinct in the wild, Arabian
oryxes have flourished in captivity and are now being
returned to their Saharan home.

PONGO JOE

Chimpanzee (*Pan troglodytes*)
Male
Born April 1, 1989
Lives in the forest of West Africa

The most intelligent of any primate except man, chimpanzees fashion tools, solve problems, even draw—but cannot concentrate for long. Chimps tend to live in small groups of several males and females with their young. When males patrol the borders of their territory, they make ferocious sounds and hostile gestures to scare off intruders, but seldom come to blows.

CREDITS

Audubon Park and Zoological Gardens, New Orleans, Louisiana
Nine-banded Armadillo
Siamang Gibbon
Tawny Owl
White Alligator

Cincinnati Zoo and Botanical Garden, Cincinnati, Ohio
Chapman's Zebra
Clouded Leopard
Indian Elephant
Lowland Gorilla
Pot-bellied Pig
Sumatran Orangutan

Denver Zoo, Denver, Colorado
Black Rhinoceros
Black-footed Penguin

Gladys Porter Zoo, Brownsville, Texas
Arabian Oryx
Cape Hunting Dog
Pygmy Hippopotamus
Reticulated Giraffe

San Diego Zoo, San Diego, California
European Roe Deer
Koala
Mountain Tapir
Nubian Ibex
Sumatran Tiger

Steve Martin's Working Wildlife, Frazier Park, California
Asian Spotted Leopard
Chimpanzee
Cinnamon Bear
Lion
Timber Wolf

ACKNOWLEDGMENTS

This project was completed in record time with the expertise and wholehearted participation of certain people. I especially want to thank Constance Sullivan, who brought the idea to me and created a beautiful book. Paula ''Kitty'' High virtually lived on the phone, arranging, coordinating, and producing the photographic sessions, and Beatriz Setti worked as my key camera assistant and companion. Gary Schneider's superb prints added immeasurably to the quality of the photographic reproduction. Alex Castro's elegant design and Carolyn Fireside's text enhance the pictures. Kate DeWitt made helpful suggestions about the text. Sarah Oliphant Studios painted the beautiful canvas backdrops that became the animals sets. Christopher Kahley made order out of the postproduction chaos. Diane Reverand, publisher of Villard Books, was enthusiastic and supportive from the beginning. Chris Peterson of the San Diego Zoo was a guide and teacher for all.

We are grateful to the following zoo directors, marketing and public relations staffs, curators, and animal handlers for making the babies available to be photographed. Clayton Freiheit, Tom Peterson, Cheryl Garrett, Cindy Bickel, Roger Milstrey, Archie Paulson, and Dr. David Kenny, VMD, of the Denver Zoo; Edward J. Maruska, Susan Silver, Cathy Hitz, Steve Romo, Mike Dulaney, Gilbert Jackson, Cecil Jackson, Sr., Pat Callahan, Denny Acus, Paul Reinhart, Carol Schottelkotte, and Dawn Strasser of the Cincinnati Zoo and Botanical Garden; L. Ronald Forman, Curt Burnette, Patrice Bell, Eve Watts, Sally Farrell, Jeff Vaccaro, and Penny Helmer of the Audubon Park and Zoological Gardens, New Orleans; Doug Meyers, Dr. Arthur C. Risser, Jr., Jeff Jouett, Chris Peterson, Lenna Doyle, Robin C. Greenlee, Boo Shaw, and Paul B. Jarand of the San Diego Zoo; Jerry Stones, Cindy Stones, Humberto Ramos, Charley Williams, Oscar Marroquin, Denise T. Davidson, Juan Trevino, Juan Luna, Rita Guerra, Tito Alverez, Ruben Reyna, Alex Vasquez, and Maria Peualver of the Gladys Porter Zoo in Brownsville, Texas; and Steve Martin, Donna Meyer Martin, Gayle Phelps, Rick Clark, Bill Marsh, and Kim Bonham of Steve Martin's Wildlife, Acton, California.

M.O.

Designed by Alex Castro
Set in Meridien and Zapf International with Gill Sans Outline Titling
by Monotype Composition Company, Baltimore, Maryland
Printed by Litho Specialties, Inc., St. Paul, Minnesota
Prints for reproduction were made by
Schneider/Erdman, New York, New York